3 MINUTE FRENCH

LESSONS 13 – 15

KIERAN BALL

Copyright © 2019 Kieran Ball

All rights reserved.

Bonjour et bienvenue (hello and welcome) to "3 Minute French". I'm Kieran, a language tutor based in the UK, and I wrote this book to help you to learn to speak French.

The lessons in this book lead on from the last book "3 Minute French: Lessons 10-12". The methodology will get you speaking quickly, without the struggle normally associated with language learning.

I'll not bore you with my life story or intricate details of the history of the methodology; I know you probably just want to start learning French now, so I'll let you get on with it.

Actually, I've changed my mind, I will bore you a little before we start. It's my book! I'll keep it as brief as I can though.

I've been tutoring people for over ten years on a one-to-one basis in a range of subjects. I love languages, I love learning and I love teaching. I also love chocolate, but this isn't really the place to discuss my chocoholism. I'm very lucky that I get to teach people every day. However, I can't fit everybody who asks me into my schedule so, regrettably, I end up turning a lot of people away. I wish I could teach the whole world but I'm yet to figure out a way of duplicating myself!

The next best thing is to teach through the medium of a book. So, that's what I've decided to do. If you're reading this book, then I will soon be teaching you the glorious splendour that is the French language.

Anyway, I'll stop blathering on in a minute and we'll get started with learning. But, firstly, let me just say this...

Hullabaloo!

No, I'm joking, of course, let me say this instead...

We are all human beings, which means we all possess the attributes that make us human beings. There's a wonderful quote by a man called Terence:

"I am human, and nothing that is human is alien to me"

What it means is that if one person is capable of something, then we are all capable of it, because we're all humans too. There's nothing in the world that I cannot understand if somebody before me has succeeded in understanding it. Therefore, it's only logical that since there are more than 200 million people in the world who have managed to learn to speak French, then you can learn it too!

Anyway, philosophising over. Let's begin.

Contents

LESSON 13 5

LESSON 14 31

LESSON 15 59

Merci... 104

Visit my website or follow me on Facebook, Twitter
or Instagram for more language hints and tips:
www.3minute.club/udemy
www.twitter.com/3mlanguages
www.facebook.com/3minutelanguages
www.instagram.com/3minutelanguages

LESSON 13

Let's start this lesson with a quick recap of the words and phrases we learnt in the last lesson. How do you say the following in French?

two weeks
one day
(to) hire / (to) rent
two days
a car
two months
one week
one month

If there are any words you can't remember, go back to the last lesson and have a quick review of them before you start this lesson. It's really important that you remember the words you've learnt so far before you move on to learn any more.

This word is the same as the English but it's just pronounced a little differently:

euros

It means "euros"
You pronounce it "err-oh"

How would you say these five sentences in French?

It's ten euros.

The bill is fifty euros.

It's one euro.

The wine is ten euros.

It's five euros for one day.

It's ten euros.
C'est dix euros.

The bill is fifty euros.
L'addition est cinquante euros.

It's one euro.
C'est un euro.

The wine is ten euros.
Le vin est dix euros.

It's five euros for one day.
C'est cinq euros pour un jour.

This word goes nicely with "euros":

centimes

It means "cents"
You pronounce it "son-teem"

WORD LIST SO FAR

euros – *euros*
centimes – *cents*

How would you say these three sentences in French?

It's fifty cents.

The bottle of water is sixty cents.

It's fifty cents for a bottle of water.

It's fifty cents.
C'est cinquante centimes.

The bottle of water is sixty cents.
La bouteille d'eau est soixante centimes.

It's fifty cents for a bottle of water.
C'est cinquante centimes pour une bouteille d'eau.

Here's your next word in French:

par

It means "per"
You pronounce it "par"

par

You can use "par" to mean "per" with any of the time phrases we've learnt so far.

par jour
per day

par semaine
per week

par mois
per month

par personne
per person

How would you say the following in French?

How much is it per day?

It's ten euros per week.

It's fifty euros per person.

How much is the car per week?

How much is it per day?
C'est combien par jour?

It's ten euros per week.
C'est dix euros par semaine.

It's fifty euros per person.
C'est cinquante euros par personne.

How much is the car per week?
C'est combien la voiture par semaine ?

French money

The way the French talk about how much something is, is very similar to how we do it in English.

Usually, in English, we only say the word euro, for example: "it's two euros fifty" and we don't bother saying "cents". Well, this is the same in French: c'est deux euros cinquante

On the other hand, you would use the word for "cents" (centimes) if there were no euros involved, for example, "it's twenty cents" - "c'est vingt centimes"

However, this isn't set in stone and it just depends on who is speaking. One person might choose to say "three euros twenty", another might say "three euros twenty cents" or another might just say "three twenty". It's exactly the same in French.

Additionally, the way that money is written varies from place to place. These are the following ways that I've seen money written on price labels:

€3,50

3,50€

3€50

One thing that is the same wherever you go, is that the French use a comma instead of a decimal point and a decimal point instead of a comma! So, that's why there is a comma in the prices above. And, "**three thousand euros**" would be written as **€3.000** with a decimal point!

Anyway, how would you say these two in French?

It's three euros fifty.

It's ten euros per week.

It's three euros fifty.
C'est trois euros cinquante.

It's ten euros per week.
C'est dix euros par semaine.

WORD LIST SO FAR

euros – *euros*
centimes – *cents*
par – *per*
par jour – *per day*
par semaine – *per week*
par mois – *per month*
par personne – *per person*

It's time to practise what we've learnt in this lesson. How do you say these sentences in French?

1. It's sixty euros
2. It's eighty one euros
3. It's fifty cents
4. It's twenty euros for two days
5. It's fifty-three euros
6. It's eighty-three euros
7. It's ten euros per bottle
8. It's fifty-two euros
9. It's eighty euros
10. It's thirty euros per month

1. C'est soixante euros
2. C'est quatre-vingt-un euros
3. C'est cinquante euros
4. C'est vingt euros pour deux jours
5. C'est cinquante-trois euros
6. C'est quatre-vingt-trois euros
7. C'est dix euros par bouteille
8. C'est cinquante-deux euros
9. C'est quatre-vingts euros
10. C'est trente euros par mois

Now, let's have a go at doing some reverse translations. What do these French sentences mean in English?

1. C'est vingt-et-un euros
2. C'est cinquante-et-un euros
3. C'est cinquante euros
4. C'est soixante-dix centimes
5. C'est cinquante-trois euros
6. C'est trente euros par mois
7. C'est vingt-deux euros
8. C'est quatre-vingt-deux euros
9. C'est quatre-vingt-un euros
10. C'est soixante euros

1. It's twenty-one euros
2. It's fifty-one euros
3. It's fifty euros
4. It's seventy cents
5. It's fifty-three euros
6. It's thirty euros per month
7. It's twenty-two euros
8. It's eighty-two euros
9. It's eighty one euros
10. It's sixty euros

What we're going to do now are some recap translations, which will incorporate words we learnt in the previous lessons.

1. The food here is very good
2. The leeks are very good
3. The chicken and the turkey are delicious
4. The turkey is delicious
5. I think the restaurant is fantastic
6. That is perfect
7. May I try the wine?
8. I think everybody is very nice
9. Also, I would like a coffee, please
10. Yes, it's for me

1. La nourriture ici est très bonne
2. Les poireaux sont très bons
3. Le poulet et la dinde sont délicieux
4. La dinde est délicieuse
5. Pour moi, le restaurant est fantastique
6. Ça c'est parfait
7. Puis-je essayer le vin?
8. Pour moi, tout le monde est très sympa
9. Aussi, je voudrais un café, s'il vous plaît
10. Oui, c'est pour moi

Let's now do some French to English recap translations.

1. Je voudrais une bouteille d'eau, s'il vous plaît
2. L'hôtel est terrible
3. Oui, c'est pour moi
4. Puis-je louer une voiture pour deux semaines, s'il vous plaît?
5. Je voudrais louer une voiture pour deux semaines. C'est combien?
6. Une bouteille de vin pour elle et l'addition pour moi
7. Oui, ça c'est très bon mais ce n'est pas parfait
8. Ce n'est pas très bon
9. C'est combien le poulet?
10. La dinde est parfaite et, aussi, mon café est délicieux

1. I would like a bottle of water, please
2. The hotel is terrible
3. Yes, it's for me
4. Can I hire a car for two weeks, please?
5. I would like to hire a car for two weeks. How much is it?
6. A bottle of wine for her and the bill for me
7. Yes, that is very good but it isn't perfect
8. It isn't very good
9. How much is the chicken?
10. The turkey is perfect and, also, my coffee is delicious

Let's recap all the words we've learnt so far. How did you say these words in French?

1. also
2. terrible
3. thank you
4. a car
5. that is...
6. (to) make
7. please
8. delicious
9. two months
10. for him
11. very
12. for me
13. the turkey
14. always
15. the food
16. per day
17. the chicken
18. nice
19. I think
20. (to) try
21. the bill
22. a coffee
23. the wine
24. two people
25. a month
26. a bottle of wine
27. my (plural)
28. the water
29. two days
30. aren't
31. hello
32. good evening
33. it is
34. see you soon
35. a tea
36. the (plural)
37. and
38. everything
39. for her
40. I would like
41. a carrot
42. have a good day
43. extraordinary
44. everybody

45. no
46. have a good evening
47. per
48. a leek
49. goodbye
50. goodnight
51. (to) pay
52. hi
53. beautiful
54. perfect
55. how much is it?
56. cents
57. per month
58. but
59. a
60. yes
61. (to) hire
62. absolutely
63. a bottle of water
64. per person
65. that
66. a reservation
67. my
68. good
69. are
70. a day
71. fantastic
72. excuse me
73. it isn't
74. per week
75. a week
76. isn't
77. a table
78. the restaurant
79. here
80. euros
81. is
82. can I?
83. two weeks
84. the hotel

1. aussi
2. terrible
3. merci
4. une voiture
5. ça c'est...
6. faire
7. s'il vous plaît
8. délicieux
9. deux mois
10. pour lui
11. très
12. pour moi
13. la dinde
14. toujours
15. la nourriture
16. par jour
17. le poulet
18. sympa
19. pour moi
20. essayer
21. l'addition
22. un café
23. le vin
24. deux personnes
25. un mois
26. une bouteille de vin
27. mes
28. l'eau
29. deux jours
30. ne sont pas
31. bonjour
32. bonsoir
33. c'est
34. à bientôt
35. un thé
36. les
37. et
38. tout
39. pour elle
40. je voudrais
41. une carotte
42. bonne journée
43. extraordinaire
44. tout le monde
45. non
46. bonne soirée
47. par
48. un poireau
49. au revoir
50. bonne nuit

51. payer
52. salut
53. beau
54. parfait
55. c'est combien?
56. centimes
57. par mois
58. mais
59. un
60. oui
61. louer
62. absolument
63. une bouteille
    d'eau
64. par personne
65. ça
66. une réservation
67. mon

68. bon
69. sont
70. un jour
71. fantastique
72. excusez-moi
73. ce n'est pas
74. par semaine
75. une semaine
76. n'est pas
77. une table
78. le restaurant
79. ici
80. euros
81. est
82. puis-je?
83. deux semaines
84. l'hôtel

LESSON 14

Let's start this lesson with a quick recap of the words and phrases we learnt in the last lesson. How do you say the following in French?

euros
cents
per
per day
per week
per month
per person

If there are any words you can't remember, go back to the last lesson and have a quick review of them before you start this lesson. It's really important that you remember the words you've learnt so far before you move on to learn any more.

Here's a useful question phrase:

à quelle heure

It means "(at) what time"
We don't always say "at" in English in the phrase "at what time"; sometimes we just say "what time". However, in French, you always have to say "à quelle heure"
You pronounce it "ah kell eur"

How would you say this in French?

At what time is the reservation?

At what time is the reservation?

À quelle heure est la réservation ?

Here's the most important meal of the day:

le petit-déjeuner

It means "the breakfast"
You pronounce it "ler pe-tee deh-jer-nay"

WORD LIST SO FAR

à quelle heure – *(at) what time*
le petit-déjeuner – *the breakfast*

How would you say this in French?

The breakfast here is fantastic.

The breakfast here is fantastic.

Le petit-déjeuner ici est fantastique.

How would you say this in French?

At what time is breakfast?

At what time is breakfast?
À quelle heure est le petit-déjeuner?

Did you get this translation correct ? Or did you miss out the word "le"?

In English, the sentence is "At what time is breakfast?" but, in French, you must always say "the breakfast". This means, you should really say "At what time is the breakfast?". That's why it's "le petit-déjeuner" and not just "petit-déjeuner".

How would you say these five sentences in French?

At what time is breakfast?

I think the breakfast is perfect.

The breakfast here is always absolutely delicious.

The breakfast is here.

I would like breakfast here.

At what time is breakfast?
À quelle heure est le petit-déjeuner?

I think the breakfast is perfect.
Pour moi, le petit-déjeuner est parfait.

The breakfast here is always absolutely delicious.
Le petit-déjeuner ici est toujours absolument délicieux.

The breakfast is here.
Le petit-déjeuner est ici.

I would like breakfast here.
Je voudrais le petit-déjeuner ici.

The next meal is:

le déjeuner

It means "the lunch"
You pronounce it "ler deh-jer-nay"

WORD LIST SO FAR

à quelle heure – *(at) what time*
le petit-déjeuner – *the breakfast*
le déjeuner – *the lunch*

How would you say the following four sentences in French?

What time is lunch?

Can I pay for lunch?

The lunch is terrible here.

Can I make a reservation for lunch?

What time is lunch?
À quelle heure est le déjeuner?

Can I pay for lunch?
Puis-je payer le déjeuner?

The lunch is terrible here.
Le déjeuner est terrible ici.

Can I make a reservation for lunch?
Puis-je faire une réservation pour le déjeuner?

The final meal of the day, and often the biggest, is:

le dîner

It means "the dinner"
You pronounce it "ler dee-nay"

WORD LIST SO FAR

à quelle heure – *(at) what time*
le petit-déjeuner – *the breakfast*
le déjeuner – *the lunch*
le dîner – *the dinner*

So, how would you say these sentences in French?

What time is dinner?

Can I pay for dinner?

Dinner is delicious.

The dinner here is always fantastic.

How much is the dinner here?

I think the dinner is terrible.

What time is dinner?
À quelle heure est le dîner?

Can I pay for dinner?
Puis-je payer le dîner?

Dinner is delicious.
Le dîner est délicieux.

The dinner here is always fantastic.
Le dîner ici est toujours
fantastique.

How much is the dinner here?
C'est combien le dîner ici?

I think the dinner is terrible.
Pour moi, le dîner est terrible.

It's time to practise what we've learnt in this lesson.

1. The breakfast isn't bad but the dinner is delicious
2. My lunch is absolutely perfect
3. The dinner here is terrible
4. My breakfast is here
5. For breakfast, I'd like an orange juice
6. For lunch, I'd like a baguette
7. What time is dinner?
8. The dinner is perfect
9. My breakfast is fantastic
10. The dinner is here

1. Le petit-déjeuner n'est pas mauvais mais le dîner est délicieux
2. Mon déjeuner est absolument parfait
3. Le dîner ici est terrible
4. Mon petit-déjeuner est ici
5. Pour le petit-déjeuner, je voudrais un jus d'orange
6. Pour le déjeuner, je voudrais une baguette
7. À quelle heure est le dîner?
8. Le dîner est parfait
9. Mon petit-déjeuner est fantastique
10. Le dîner est ici

Now, let's have a go at doing some reverse translations.

1. Le petit-déjeuner n'est pas mauvais mais le déjeuner est délicieux
2. Mon déjeuner est délicieux
3. Mon dîner est délicieux
4. Pour le petit-déjeuner, je voudrais un croissant
5. Mon petit-déjeuner est terrible
6. Le dîner ici est délicieux
7. Le petit-déjeuner ici est absolument fantastique
8. C'est combien le déjeuner?
9. Mon déjeuner est absolument parfait
10. Mon déjeuner est ici

1. **The breakfast isn't bad but the lunch is delicious**
2. My lunch is delicious
3. My dinner is delicious
4. For breakfast, I would like a croissant
5. My breakfast is terrible
6. The dinner here is delicious
7. The breakfast here is absolutely fantastic
8. How much is lunch?
9. My lunch is absolutely perfect
10. My lunch is here

What we're going to do now are some recap translations, which will incorporate words we learnt in the previous lessons.

1. I would like a table for four, please
2. How much is it for six days?
3. It's thirty euros per month
4. It's eighty euros
5. How much is it for four days?
6. I think it's fantastic
7. It isn't good; it's absolutely extraordinary
8. Everything is here
9. How much is it for two days?
10. Excuse me, the bill, please

1. Je voudrais une table pour quatre, s'il vous plaît
2. C'est combien pour six jours?
3. C'est trente euros par mois
4. C'est quatre-vingts euros
5. C'est combien pour quatre jours?
6. Pour moi, c'est fantastique
7. Ce n'est pas bon; c'est absolument extraordinaire
8. Tout est ici
9. C'est combien pour deux jours?
10. Excusez-moi, l'addition, s'il vous plaît

Let's now do some French to English recap translations.

1. Ce n'est pas pour elle; c'est pour moi
2. Je voudrais une table pour trois personnes, s'il vous plaît
3. Oui, c'est pour moi, merci
4. Ce n'est pas fantastique mais c'est très bon
5. Un café pour moi
6. Ma dinde est parfaite
7. Je voudrais essayer le vin, s'il vous plaît
8. C'est huit cent euros
9. Ça c'est ma dinde
10. Puis-je essayer le poulet, s'il vous plaît?

1. It isn't for her; it's for me
2. I'd like a table for three people, please
3. Yes, it's for me, thank you
4. It isn't fantastic but it's very good
5. A coffee for me
6. My turkey is perfect
7. I'd like to try the wine, please
8. It's eight hundred euros
9. That's my turkey
10. Can I try the chicken, please?

Let's recap all the words we've learnt so far. How did you say these words in French?

1. a bottle of wine
2. please
3. goodbye
4. hello
5. hi
6. and
7. it is
8. (the) dinner
9. always
10. is
11. yes
12. per person
13. are
14. my
15. have a good evening
16. the turkey
17. two days
18. the (plural)
19. have a good day
20. here
21. isn't
22. perfect
23. the water
24. for me
25. thank you
26. beautiful
27. no
28. everybody
29. a bottle of water
30. nice
31. (to) hire
32. good evening
33. per month
34. (to) pay
35. it isn't
36. a week
37. a month
38. fantastic
39. extraordinary
40. (the) breakfast
41. for her
42. at what time
43. the wine
44. the bill
45. the restaurant

46. goodnight
47. a day
48. two weeks
49. a carrot
50. per week
51. a tea
52. (the) lunch
53. per
54. can I?
55. aren't
56. that
57. two people
58. a reservation
59. a
60. but
61. my (plural)
62. excuse me
63. good
64. for him
65. euros
66. I would like
67. a car
68. how much is it?
69. the hotel
70. cents
71. also
72. two months
73. a coffee
74. a leek
75. absolutely
76. (to) try
77. see you soon
78. the food
79. per day
80. the chicken
81. a table
82. very
83. that is...
84. (to) make
85. I think
86. terrible
87. everything
88. delicious

1. une bouteille de vin
2. s'il vous plaît
3. au revoir
4. bonjour
5. salut
6. et
7. c'est
8. le dîner
9. toujours
10. est
11. oui
12. par personne
13. sont
14. mon
15. bonne soirée
16. la dinde
17. deux jours
18. les
19. bonne journée
20. ici
21. n'est pas
22. parfait
23. l'eau
24. pour moi
25. merci
26. beau
27. non
28. tout le monde
29. une bouteille d'eau
30. sympa
31. louer
32. bonsoir
33. par mois
34. payer
35. ce n'est pas
36. une semaine
37. un mois
38. fantastique
39. extraordinaire
40. le petit-déjeuner
41. pour elle
42. à quelle heure
43. le vin
44. l'addition
45. le restaurant
46. bonne nuit
47. un jour
48. deux semaines
49. une carotte
50. par semaine

51. un thé
52. le déjeuner
53. par
54. puis-je?
55. ne sont pas
56. ça
57. deux personnes
58. une réservation
59. un
60. mais
61. mes
62. excusez-moi
63. bon
64. pour lui
65. euros
66. je voudrais
67. une voiture
68. c'est combien?
69. l'hôtel
70. centimes
71. aussi
72. deux mois
73. un café
74. un poireau
75. absolument
76. essayer
77. à bientôt
78. la nourriture
79. par jour
80. le poulet
81. une table
82. très
83. ça c'est...
84. faire
85. pour moi
86. terrible
87. tout
88. délicieux

LESSON 15

Let's start this lesson with a quick recap of the words and phrases we learnt in the last lesson. How do you say the following in French?

(at) what time
the breakfast
the lunch
the dinner

If there are any words you can't remember, go back to the last lesson and have a quick review of them before you start this lesson. It's really important that you remember the words you've learnt so far before you move on to learn any more.

This lesson is going to be all about telling the time. Here's your first time related phrase:

à ... heures

It means "at ... o'clock"
You pronounce it "ah ... eur"
You can put any number in between the "à" and the "heures"

How would you say these four sentences in French?

At three o'clock.

It is at five o'clock.

Dinner is at eight o'clock.

Breakfast is at seven o'clock.

At three o'clock.
À trois heures.

It is at five o'clock.
C'est à cinq heures.

Dinner is at eight o'clock.
Le dîner est à huit heures.

Breakfast is at seven o'clock.
Le petit-déjeuner est à sept heures.

7am vs. 7pm

There are no words for a.m. or p.m. in French, but they do have two ways of differentiating between the two. Either you can use the 24 hour clock, which the French do a lot, or you can use these two phrases:

le matin
(in the morning)

le soir
(in the evening)

You can put these two phrases after you say the time, for example:

c'est à huit heures le matin
it's at 8am

c'est à huit heures le soir
it's at 8pm

Or, to show that you mean pm, you could use the 24 hour clock. For example:

c'est à vingt heures
it's at 8pm (20:00)

WORD LIST SO FAR

à...heures – *at...o'clock*
le matin – *am (in the morning)*
le soir – *pm (in the evening)*

How would you say this in French using the 24 hour clock?

Dinner is at eight o'clock.

Dinner is at eight o'clock.
Le dîner est à vingt heures.

How would you say these two sentences in French?

Breakfast is at 7am.

Dinner is at 5pm.

Breakfast is at 7am.
Le petit-déjeuner est à sept heures le matin.

Dinner is at 5pm.
Le dîner est à cinq heures le soir.

This phrase is similar to the last phrase we learnt but with a little extra bit:

à ... heures et demie

It means "at half past ..." and you can put any number on the dots
You pronounce it "ah ... eur ay der-mee"

WORD LIST SO FAR

à...heures – *at...o'clock*
à...heures et demie – *at half past...*
le matin – *am (in the morning)*
le soir – *pm (in the evening)*

How would you say the following three sentences in French?

Lunch is at half past two.

It's at half past five.

The reservation is at half past three.

Lunch is at half past two.
Le déjeuner est à deux heures et demie.

It's at half past five.
C'est à cinq heures et demie.

The reservation is at half past three.
La réservation est à trois heures et demie.

How would you say this using the 24 hour clock?

It's at half past two. (14:30)

It's at half past two.
C'est à quatorze heures et demie.

Let's add another time phrase:

à ... heures et quart

It means "at quarter past..." and, again, you can put
any number where the dots are
You pronounce it "ah ... eur ay car"

WORD LIST SO FAR

à...heures – *at...o'clock*
à...heures et demie – *at half past...*
le matin – *am (in the morning)*
le soir – *pm (in the evening)*
à...heures et quart – *at quarter past...*

How would you say the six sentences below in French?

Lunch is at quarter past two.

It's at quarter past four.

I would like to make a reservation at quarter past seven.

It's at 17:15.

My reservation is at 6:15pm.

Breakfast is at quarter past eight in the morning.

Lunch is at quarter past two.
Le déjeuner est à deux heures et quart.

It's at quarter past four.
C'est à quatre heures et quart.

I would like to make a reservation at quarter past seven.
Je voudrais faire une réservation à sept heures et quart.

It's at 17:15.
C'est à dix-sept heures et quart.

My reservation is at 6:15pm.
Ma réservation est à six heures et quart le soir.

Breakfast is at quarter past eight in the morning.
Le petit-déjeuner est à huit heures et quart le matin.

Let's add another time phrase:

à ... heures moins le quart

It means "at quarter to..." and, as always, you can
put any number where the dots are
You pronounce it "ah ... eur mwan(g) ler car"

WORD LIST SO FAR

à...heures – *at...o'clock*
à...heures et demie – *at half past...*
le matin – *am (in the morning)*
le soir – *pm (in the evening)*
à...heures et quart – *at quarter past...*
à...heures moins le quart – *at quarter to...*

How would you say these four sentences in French?

My reservation is at quarter to eight.

Lunch is at quarter to two.

It's at quarter to seven.

Dinner is at quarter to seven.

My reservation is at quarter to eight.
Ma réservation est à huit heures moins le quart.

Lunch is at quarter to two.
Le déjeuner est à deux heures moins le quart.

It's at quarter to seven.
C'est à sept heures moins le quart.

Dinner is at quarter to seven.
Le dîner est à dix-neuf heures moins le quart.

When you want to ask somebody what the time is right now, you can use this useful question:

Quelle heure est-il?

It means "What time is it?"
You pronounce it "kel eur eh-teel"

WORD LIST SO FAR

à...heures – *at...o'clock*
à...heures et demie – *at half past...*
le matin – *am (in the morning)*
le soir – *pm (in the evening)*
à...heures et quart – *at quarter past...*
à...heures moins le quart – *at quarter to...*
quelle heure est-il ? – *what time is it ?*

How would you say this in French?

Excuse me, what time is it?

Excuse me, what time is it?

Excusez-moi, quelle heure est-il ?

What time is it right now?

All of the time phrases I've given you above mean "at" a specific time. They all start with the word "à". However, if you want to say what time it is right now, there's a slightly different way of saying "it is".

Here's the phrase: il est ... heures
It means: it is ... o'clock

When you're telling somebody what time it is right now, you must say "il est" for "it is" and you don't say the little "à" that we've seen in all the time phrases we've looked at in this lesson. Look at the examples below:

il est sept heures
it is seven o'clock

il est sept heures et quart
it is quarter past seven

il est sept heures moins le quart
it is quarter to seven

il est sept heures et demie
it is half past seven

WORD LIST SO FAR

à...heures – *at...o'clock*
à...heures et demie – *at half past...*
le matin – *am (in the morning)*
le soir – *pm (in the evening)*
à...heures et quart – *at quarter past...*
à...heures moins le quart – *at quarter to...*
quelle heure est-il ? – *what time is it ?*
il est...heures – *it is...o'clock (right now)*

How would you say these three sentences in French?

It is four o'clock.

It is half past nine.

It is 2pm.

It is four o'clock.
Il est quatre heures.

It is half past nine.
Il est neuf heures et demie.

It is 2pm.
Il est deux heures le soir.

Writing the time

In English, you usually use a colon to write the time. For example:

5:45pm
16:15
20:05

However, in French, instead of using a colon, you use a lower case 'h'. So, the times I've put above would be written like this:

17h45
16h15
20h05

The little 'h' stands for 'heures'.

Other times

In this lesson, we've learnt how to say o'clock, half past, quarter past, and quarter to. But, what about the other times, like five past or twenty past?

Well, in French, you always start by saying "...heures" and then you add anything else onto the end.

For anything **past** the hour, you just add it on. So, "five past seven" would be "sept heures cinq". For anything **to** the hour, you use the word "moins", which means "less" or "minus". So, "five to seven" would be "sept heures moins cinq" (literally meaning "seven hours minus five").

On the opposite page, I've listed most of the common times. You can change the seven or eight to any number you like.

07h00 - sept heures
07h05 - sept heures cinq
07h10 - sept heures dix
07h15 - sept heures et quart
07h20 - sept heures vingt
07h25 - sept heures vingt-cinq
07h30 - sept heures et demie
07h35 - huit heures moins vingt-cinq
07h40 - huit heures moins vingt
07h45 - huit heures moins le quart
07h50 - huit heures moins dix
07h55 - huit heures moins cinq
08h00 - huit heures

I've drawn a little clock for you to use to help you to tell the time in French. Well, I didn't draw it, I used a computer to make it, but the sentiment still remains.

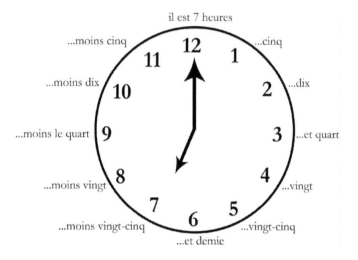

Just remember, whenever you want to say that something is "at" a specific time, you must say "à" in front of the time. If you just want to say what time it is now, you don't need to bother with the "à" but you would use "il est" for "it is".

WORD LIST SO FAR

à...heures – *at...o'clock*
à...heures et demie – *at half past...*
le matin – *am (in the morning)*
le soir – *pm (in the evening)*
à...heures et quart – *at quarter past...*
à...heures moins le quart – *at quarter to...*
quelle heure est-il ? – *what time is it ?*
il est...heures – *it is...o'clock (right now)*

It's time to practise what we've learnt in this lesson.

1. At half past two
2. It's at quarter past nine
3. It's at quarter to eight
4. It's half past four
5. It's quarter to three
6. It's at half past four
7. It's at quarter to six
8. It's half past five
9. Dinner is at eight o'clock
10. It's two o'clock

1. À deux heures et demie
2. C'est à neuf heures et quart
3. C'est à huit heures moins le quart
4. Il est quatre heures et demie
5. Il est trois heures moins le quart
6. C'est à quatre heures et demie
7. C'est à six heures moins le quart
8. Il est cinq heures et demie
9. Le dîner est à huit heures
10. Il est deux heures

Now, let's have a go at doing some reverse translations.

1. C'est à six heures et quart
2. Il est deux heures et quart
3. Le déjeuner est à trois heures
4. C'est à sept heures moins le quart
5. C'est à neuf heures
6. C'est à neuf heures et demie
7. Il est douze heures
8. C'est à deux heures
9. C'est à douze heures
10. Il est dix heures moins dix

1. It's at quarter past six
2. It's quarter past two
3. Lunch is at three o'clock
4. It's at quarter to seven
5. It's at nine o'clock
6. It's at half past nine
7. It is twelve o'clock
8. It's at two o'clock
9. It's at twelve o'clock
10. It's ten to ten

Let's now do some recap translations..

1. I would like a tea for me and a coffee for her, please
2. Can I hire a car for two weeks, please?
3. It isn't good
4. The chicken is very good but the turkey is extraordinary
5. The restaurant is very good
6. I think my lunch is fantastic
7. My breakfast is here
8. I would like a reservation for three people, please
9. My hotel is terrible but the restaurant is extraordinary
10. The breakfast is absolutely fantastic here

1. Je voudrais un thé pour moi et un café pour elle, s'il vous plaît
2. Puis-je louer une voiture pour deux semaines, s'il vous plaît?
3. Ce n'est pas bon
4. Le poulet est très bon mais la dinde est extraordinaire
5. Le restaurant est très bon
6. Pour moi, mon déjeuner est fantastique
7. Mon petit-déjeuner est ici
8. Je voudrais une réservation pour trois personnes, s'il vous plaît
9. Mon hôtel est terrible mais le restaurant est extraordinaire
10. Le petit-déjeuner est absolument fantastique ici

Let's now do some French to English recap translations.

1. Je voudrais une bouteille de vin. C'est combien?
2. Ça ce n'est pas ma dinde
3. Le vin est quatre euros
4. Je voudrais une table pour deux, s'il vous plaît
5. Mon poulet est parfait
6. La dinde est parfaite
7. Je voudrais trois cafés et deux thés, s'il vous plaît. C'est combien?
8. C'est absolument extraordinaire ici
9. Non, merci
10. C'est dix euros par bouteille

1. I would like a bottle of wine. How much is it?
2. That isn't my turkey
3. The wine is four euros
4. I would like a table for two, please
5. My chicken is perfect
6. The turkey is perfect
7. I would like three coffees and two teas, please. How much is it?
8. It's absolutely extraordinary here
9. No, thank you
10. It's ten euros per bottle

Let's recap all the words we've learnt so far. How did you say these words in French?

1. a bottle of wine
2. a table
3. that
4. the bill
5. excuse me
6. (to) pay
7. how much is it?
8. can I?
9. per day
10. terrible
11. two weeks
12. two months
13. a week
14. goodbye
15. are
16. it isn't
17. it is...o'clock
18. for him
19. it is
20. have a good day
21. (to) try
22. nice
23. a reservation
24. I would like
25. the restaurant
26. is
27. extraordinary
28. hi
29. the food
30. very
31. and
32. perfect
33. the wine
34. aren't
35. absolutely
36. (to) hire
37. everything
38. per month
39. (at)...o'clock
40. a tea
41. the chicken
42. euros
43. for her
44. the turkey
45. a month
46. that is...

47. my
48. (at) quarter past...
49. two people
50. goodnight
51. hello
52. (at) quarter to...
53. my (plural)
54. a carrot
55. I think
56. per
57. a
58. (the) breakfast
59. a coffee
60. a bottle of water
61. here
62. (the) dinner
63. fantastic
64. have a good evening
65. a leek
66. a car
67. (to) make
68. the hotel
69. the (plural)
70. (at) half past...
71. two days
72. yes
73. good evening
74. always
75. per person
76. but
77. a day
78. delicious
79. everybody
80. also
81. good
82. no
83. beautiful
84. at what time
85. cents
86. isn't
87. thank you
88. please
89. what time is it?
90. the water
91. see you soon
92. for me
93. (the) lunch
94. per week

1. une bouteille de vin
2. une table
3. ça
4. l'addition
5. excusez-moi
6. payer
7. c'est combien?
8. puis-je?
9. par jour
10. terrible
11. deux semaines
12. deux mois
13. une semaine
14. au revoir
15. sont
16. ce n'est pas
17. il est...heures
18. pour lui
19. c'est
20. bonne journée
21. essayer
22. sympa
23. une réservation
24. je voudrais
25. le restaurant
26. est
27. extraordinaire
28. salut
29. la nourriture
30. très
31. et
32. parfait
33. le vin
34. ne sont pas
35. absolument
36. louer
37. tout
38. par mois
39. (à)...heures
40. un thé
41. le poulet
42. euros
43. pour elle
44. la dinde
45. un mois
46. ça c'est...
47. mon
48. (à)...heures et quart

49. deux personnes
50. bonne nuit
51. bonjour
52. (à)...heures moins le quart
53. mes
54. une carotte
55. pour moi
56. par
57. un
58. le petit-déjeuner
59. un café
60. une bouteille d'eau
61. ici
62. le dîner
63. fantastique
64. bonne soirée
65. un poireau
66. une voiture
67. faire
68. l'hôtel
69. les
70. (à)...heures et demie
71. deux jours
72. oui
73. bonsoir
74. toujours
75. par personne
76. mais
77. un jour
78. délicieux
79. tout le monde
80. aussi
81. bon
82. non
83. beau
84. à quelle heure
85. centimes
86. n'est pas
87. merci
88. s'il vous plaît
89. quelle heure est-il?
90. l'eau
91. à bientôt
92. pour moi
93. le déjeuner
94. par semaine

Merci

Before you go, I'd like to say "merci" for buying this book. There are lots of French books available and you chose to read mine, so I am eternally grateful for that.

I hope you have enjoyed this book and I hope you're glad you made the purchase. I also hope you've started to realise how easy learning a new language can be.

This book contained lessons thirteen to fifteen of my "3 Minute French" course. If you would like to learn more, you can get the next book in the series containing lessons sixteen to eighteen, and further books after that to continue building your French language skills.

For more information on where to get the next books, or if you'd like any more tips on language learning, you can visit my website www.3minute.club/udemy

You can also follow me on Twitter, Facebook or Instagram:

www.twitter.com/3mlanguages

www.facebook.com/3minutelanguages

www.instagram.com/3minutelanguages

If you liked this book, you might also like my other language course series:

3 Minute Languages

The 3 Minute Languages courses are perfect for the complete beginner. They will get you speaking a language from scratch, assuming you know absolutely nothing. You will be amazed at how quickly you're able to put sentences together. And you will memorise new words and phrases easily without even trying.

Building Structures

The Building Structures courses are a revolutionary way to look at foreign language acquisition; you will learn how any language can be broken down into around fifteen structures. Each course focuses on a different structure, and you will learn how to form it, make it negative and turn it into a question. Each structure gives you a huge amount to say, and once you've learnt all fifteen structures, you will know everything about the language. All you have to do is fill in the gaps with words to form a sentence. These courses are for students who are slightly familiar with the language, and what to boost their progress.

Quick Guides

The Quick Guides are grammar guides. I recommend these for students who have already been learning the language, and would like to accelerate your learning. The Quick Guides are perfect for anybody who wants an in-depth look at a specific grammar point within the language.

You can get discounts on all of my courses on Udemy by using the discount code **3MINUTE** on checkout. Find the full list here: www.3minute.club/udemy

Thank you again, merci et à bientôt!

Printed in Great Britain
by Amazon